Debate Handbook

The Smart Way to Exercise the Mind!

Volume 1
RELIGION & POLITICS

Michelle J. Dyett-Welcome

In collaboration with Dwain G. Welcome,
Maheem J. Welcome and Matteel S. Welcome

Smart Publishing House
Far Rockaway, NY 11691
www.smartpublishinghouse.com

Dwain G. Welcome, Editor

First Published by
Smart House Publishing 11/28/15

ISBN-13: 978-0692590270
ISBN-10: 0692590277

Printed in the United States of America
Far Rockaway, New York

Printed on acid-free paper.

SMART
PUBLISHING
...the smart place to publish HOUSE

TABLE OF CONTENTS

• • •

ACKNOWLEDGEMENTS

First, I give God thanks and praise for making this book a reality. He is an awesome God! He has blessed me with creative ability and has poured upon me the richness of his glory through Jesus Christ.

To my family Dwain, Maheem and Matteel, thank you for your support and impute. You have contributed so much to the joy in my life and to the fruition of this book. My heart is filled with love and appreciation.

To my critique, buddy John, thank you for your suggestions, questions and assistance as I worked on this project.

INTRODUCTION

Once considered the purview of the elite, debates are finding their way back into schools and into the homes of homeschoolers. The debating process teaches children how to investigate, think critically, logically, and to analyze information in order to put forth a sound argument.

It is our intent to help students—regardless of age to be able to develop sound opinions in order to sharpen and expand their mind.

This book has two debate topics religion and politics, which are usually hot button topics, because they stir up peoples passions.

In chapter 4, you will find the self-assessment section; it will help you, explore who you are and what you want from your life. This is vital in order for you to feel more comfortable in life, in making decisions, or in defending your debate position.

Here is to your debating success!

CHAPTER 1

ARE YOU READY TO DEBATE?

Don't raise your voice, improve your argument.

Desmond Tutu

*It is better to debate a question without settling
it than to settle a question without debating it.*

Joseph Joubert

What is a Debate?

Debating is a natural way to help young people expand their minds. It helps them to think critically and to expand their viewpoint.

A debate is a discussion, which explores the two sides to a position. It promotes learning, increases knowledge, and in some cases helps the participants to grow in wisdom.

A debate consists of five steps . . . gather information, explore all sides of an issue, form an opinion, defend your position, and refine your position in light of new evidence.

Many confuse debating with arguing, but a debate is an exercise to expand your mind or to refine your position or thinking, while an argument is trying to win at all costs and it does not always involve listening.

Whole Class

If you are a teacher or a home schooling parent, you can use this book to spark excitement and enthusiasm in your students. As you read the debate prompts and do the research together, you can model what it means to be an active and engaged reader. Ask questions, search for answers, share comments about what you discover aloud. This will keep everyone alert and involved.

Whole Family

The exercises in this book are great activities for family night. The whole family can be involved. Choose debate teams. Select a debate topic. Do the necessary research during the week. Schedule a debate night. Then have fun as you present your position and refine it as needed.

Individual Time/Paired Readings

Students can work both independently or in pairs. There are times when it will be best for them to work alone. While at other times it would be helpful for them to work in pairs for this will help to sharpen their critical thinking skills, gather more information, and to practice their reasoning and debating skills.

New Words

During the information, gathering stage students may encounter new words. They should make note of these words and their definitions.

New Word	Official Definition	Used in a Sentence	My Definition

Before and After Debate

Write down your debate topic this will help to keep it clear and fresh in your mind. Keep track of how your opinion changes through the process.

Does your opinion get stronger, has your opinion changed, or does your opinion remain the same?

Debate Topic: My debate topic is…

Before Debate: These are my opinions about the topic before research…

After Debate: These are my opinions about the topic after research…

Reasons Why: After doing research, this is how my opinion has changed…

Look at Both Sides

As you go through the debate process, remember to look at both sides. You should be able to present either side—for the issue or against the issue—equally well.

Debate Topic:

For the Issue	Against the Issue

Listen

When your opponent is speaking, pay attention and actively listen to what he/she is saying. The information that is shared may have an impact on your position—it could strengthen it or it can reveal a weakness (flaw) in your argument.

Take Notes

While your opponent is speaking take notes that are relevant to your position or that will influence your opinion on the matter.

Preparation Time

If you are using the debate prompts for debates and not for impromptu speeches, more time will be needed for students to prepare for the debate.

If you are a homeschooler, it is recommended that you allow an hour to seven days for preparation.

If you are a teacher, assigning debate topics to your class it is recommended that you allow one to seven days for proper preparation.

CHAPTER 2

Debate Topic 1

RELIGION

A thorough knowledge of the Bible is worth more than a college education.

Theodore Roosevelt

Question 1

Can evolution and creation coexist?

Background

The theory of evolution attempts to explain how man came to be as it advances the notion that God had nothing to do with the process, if indeed he does exist.

Evolutionist have used many theories to try and clarify how humans came about including the theistic evolution, the day-age theory, the gap theory, and the progressive creation theory. Although each theory presents a unique argument they all have one thing in common, that God (if there is a God) created a less than perfect world and in order for it to become better it needed to evolve.

Creationism on the other hand relies on the Bible for its account of how man came into existence. Creationist believe that man's appearance on the earth is due to an active and involved God.

As creationist, they believe the whole Word of God and are not willing to choose sections of the Bible to believe while rejecting others.

YES

The evolutionist for this position believe that there is common ground upon which creationists and evolutionist can coexist. It requires an amendment of the unequivocal belief that the biblical account of creation is accurate and complete.

NO

The creationist who oppose this positon believe that what they believe is true. That evolution is a fairytale and the only truth as to the origin of man is found in the Bible.

Therefore, no common ground exists upon which the two sides can agree or coexist.

Is there any way that these two warring factions can ever coexist. One side believes they have truth, while the other has deception.

Now What's Your Point of View?

Question 2

Should Christians bear arms in times of war?

Background

Many Christian's have objected to participating in the war because it violated their moral beliefs or religious convictions.

YES

Those that argue the affirmative believe that citizens should submit to the authority of the government—who decides issues of war.

NO

Those opposed would contend that war goes against God's principals and therefore God's law should prevail—*"Thou shall not kill" Exodus 20:13, NIV*.

Now What's Your Point of View?

Question 3

Is the Bible accurate?

Background

Over the centuries, many have contended that the Bible is not accurate for men wrote it and therefore there must be inconsistencies within the book.

However, others believe that the Bible is an inspired book, by an infallible and holy God therefore, it contains no inconsistencies.

YES

The proponents believe that the Bible the inspired word of God written though men— under the leading of the Spirit of God and is therefore accurate and infallible.

NO

Opponents believe that the Bible is a good storybook written by men and has flaws and thus is not completely accurate and should not be used as an authoritative book.

Now What's Your Point of View?

Question 4

Can humans really end the world?

Background

Many believe that man is heading toward total destruction. They contend that man is going to self-destruct because of war and their neglect of global changes. Others believe that the world will be destroyed but by the hand of God and not man.

YES

Those who hold this view believe that humans will be responsible for destroying the world and life, as we know it through wars.

NO

Those who argue against this position believe that man does not have the power or authority to destroy the world. That God alone has that right and ability.

Now What's Your Point of View?

Question 5

Is the Devil real?

Background

The reality of the devil has long been questioned. Many do not believe that there is a real devil—but rather believe that people act and operate in an evil way, which is devilish.

YES

People who argue the affirmative believe that the devil is the archangel Lucifer who was kicked out of heaven because of his rebellion and his contention to take the throne of God.

NO

Those who argue the negative believe that there is no devil. That there are only humans who operate in an evil way against fellow human beings.

Now What's Your Point of View?

• • •

Question 6

Are men inherently good?

Background

This has been an age long debate going back to man's beginning. Are humans born with a natural tendency towards good? Is goodness inherently in their nature?

YES

Those for this position believe that when man is born they only know how to be good and that it is their nature to do and be good.

NO

Those for this position believe that man is not born good therefore, they are not inherently good. They are evil by nature and have to learn how to be good.

Now What's Your Point of View?

Question 7

Are all religions equal?

Background

Most religions are based on the worship of a higher being. Therefore, the argument has been made that all religions are equal. They have the commonality of a supreme god that deserves worship.

YES

Those for this position believe that no one-god is higher or more valid than any other god thus making all religions equal and lawful.

NO

Those opposed believe that all religions are not equal, because not all gods are equal. There is one supreme God; therefore, not all religions are equal.

Now What's Your Point of View?

Question 8

Do all religions lead to God?

Background

This question has been debated over the years. The universalism of religion and the worship of a higher being have helped to advance the belief that all religions lead to God.

YES

Those who support this position believe that all paths lead to God and that there is more than "one way" reach God.

NO

Those who support this position believe that all paths do not lead to God. They believe that there is only one path that leads to God— Jesus.

Now What's Your Point of View?

Question 9

What is evil?

Background

Many things have been defined as evil, the actions of a leader, the collective acts of a mob, even the cruelty of a parent—but do these constitute evil?

Evil has long been associated with the devil—those things that are cruel or destructive.

What is evil? Does evil really exist?

YES

Proponents of this position believe evil exists, that it is the fruit of the devil who to robs, kills and destroys.

NO

The opposition believe that evil is the self-serving choices of men who seek to advance his self-benefiting agenda. It is not related to or caused by the devil but rather by the selfish and wicked acts of man.

Now What's Your Point of View?

Question 10

Is truth relative? Is there absolute truth?

Background

In today's ever-changing moral climate, many believe that there is no one, singular, or true answer to the vast number of situations that confront an individual. All truth is relative and subject to time, place, and individual preferences.

Some argue that absolute truth does exist for all matters and in all situations. There are defined "rights' and "wrongs" to all ethical questions which confront man. Therefore, truth is not subjective or prone to change.

YES

Proponents assert, "Truth is both relative and absolute" based upon situational ethics and individual preferences. All truth is relative to the person, time and place in which they reside.

A person's personal preference is truth for example he may believe, "Fruit and Nut are the best chocolates ever made."

Cultural etiquette is also truth for example, in the United States, it is culturally acceptable to keep ones shoes on, but in Japan, it is frowned upon.

NO

Proponents of this position assert that truth is absolute. They contend that what is true for one person is true for another person in similar circumstances.

These truths are reflected in the fact that all humans need food and water to exist. Alternatively, that the laws of gravity apply to everyone and everything on the planet.

Now What's Your Point of View?

Question 11

Is spiritualism a true religion?

Background

Spiritualism the belief that god exists but that man can communicate with the dead through a medium.

Religion on the other hand is an organized approach to human spirituality. Is spiritualism a religion?

YES

Those in favor of this position believe that spiritualism is a religion because it holds that there is a god who is at the center of their belief system—and their practices are based on beliefs and teachings that they hold sacred.

NO

Those in favor of this position believe that spiritualism is not a religion for there is only one true religion—the worship of God through Jesus—and communication with the dead is expressly forbidden. Thus, spiritualism is a false religion.

Now What's Your Point of View?

Question 12

Is spiritualism the same as Christianity?

Background

Many spiritualists share a common belief with the Christian faith that there is a power beyond human beings that influence the world and those within it.

For Christians that power is the Godhead—represented by God the Father, the Son Jesus Christ and God the Holy Spirit.

For spiritualist that force can come in a number of forms—including the universe, mother earth, the sun, the moon, spirits and various deities.

YES

Those that say "yes" may argue that as spiritualists we accept the Bible and believe that Jesus lived and taught on the earth showing us the way in which we should live.

NO

Those that say "no" may argue that the two are not the same because unlike spiritualism Christianity relies on the ministry of Jesus Christ who walked the earth in flesh, was crucified, and was raised from the dead.

Furthermore, they believe that Jesus was fully God and fully man and there is only one true God. At the core of Christianity is the fact that Jesus is not just a teacher but also the savior.

Now What's Your Point of View?

Question 13

Is spiritualism good for those who practice it?

Background

Many contend that spiritualism is destructive—for those who practice it, for their communities and for their nations.

Those who practice spiritualism believe that the spirits bless them if they follow what they are commanded to do.

YES

Those who argue the affirmative believe that spiritualism allows you to be one with the universe and allows you to tap into a source beyond the limitations of the physical.

NO

Those that argue the negative believe that spiritualism is detrimental to the individual, their communities, and their nation because it allows people under demonic influence to operate outside the realm of accountability or acceptable human behavior, blinding them from eternal truths, and preventing them from getting to know the One true God, Yahweh.

Now What's Your Point of View?

Question 14

Are demons real?

Background

Many believe that demons are real and that they are fallen angels that are intent on destroying men.

While others believe that, they are guides and helpers that are willing to guide men through life—and are not demons but are angels of light. There are those who believe that demons do not exist at all.

YES

Those that argue "yes" believe that demons are angels, which were tossed out of heaven to the earth and are under the command of Satan the fallen archangel whose mission is to rob, kill, and destroy.

NO

Those who argue "no" believe that demons do not exist, but rather all angels are angels of light who act as guides helping humankind as they go through life.

Now What's Your Point of View?

Question 15

Is hell a real place?

Background

Christians and others believe hell is the place where evil and sinful people go after they die for eternity. While others believe that, men are reincarnated and do not go to hell.

YES

The proponents of this position argue that the Word of God states that hell is a real place created for Satan and his angels and for those who follow him.

NO

Opponents will argue that hell is not real for man is reincarnated, thus allowing him to enjoy many lifetimes.

Now What's Your Point of View?

Religion is what keeps the poor from murdering the rich.

Napoleon Bonaparte

Idea Prompts

In this section (questions 16-25), you will be given a question for which **you are to gather the background information through research.**

Identify the strongest arguments for each position and list it. Then give your point of view.

Try to narrow down the *yes* and *no* position to one argument that reflects the general trend of each position—this will reduce confusion and the blurring of the issue.

Question 16

Do demons influence music inciting depraved thinking, antisocial behavior, or lewdness?

Background

YES

NO

Now What's Your Point of View?

Question 17

Can demons influence people through movies? Do they influence the viewer to become lustful, criminally minded, or even violent?

Background

YES

NO

Now What's Your Point of View?

Question 18

Can demons influence people through television, by reprograming them through subliminal messages, which can affect their behavior, thoughts, emotions, or desires?

Background

YES

NO

Now What's Your Point of View?

Question 19

Can demons influence through the arts by causing artist to cast spells or incantations on objects in order to influence the unsuspecting owner of such creative works?

Background

YES

NO

Now What's Your Point of View?

Question 20

Do demons attend Christian churches in order to destroy the fellowship or a godly standard through political correctness in place of honesty, truth, or love?

Background

YES

NO

Now What's Your Point of View?

Question 21

Can Christians have demons dwelling inside of them?

Background

YES

NO

Now What's Your Point of View?

Question 22

Is there witchcraft or doctrines of demons active in the Christian church?

Background

YES

NO

Now What's Your Point of View?

Question 23

Can demons control men, rule their thoughts, or control their bodies?

Background

YES

NO

Now What's Your Point of View?

Question 24

Are familiar spirits friend or foe? Are they helpful guides or sinister beings intent on the destruction of men?

Background

YES

NO

Now What's Your Point of View?

Question 25

Can the dead really talk to the living? Or are these creatures familiar spirits intent on deceiving hurting and desperate people?

Background

YES

NO

Now What's Your Point of View?

CHAPTER 3

Debate Topic 2

POLITICS

One of the reasons people hate politics is that truth is rarely a politician's objective. Election and power are.

Cal Thomas

Question 1

Should candidates be judged by their character and private lives?

Background

On many occasions, political campaigns revolve around the personal misconduct of individuals seeking or holding office. Even though these individuals may be qualified and have professional experience to carry out their duties. Should personal indiscretions disqualify them from holding political offices?

YES

Those that argue the affirmative believe that one's character is an indication of how one carries out one's responsibility.

NO

Those opposed would argue that politicians should be entitled to the same privacy that ordinary citizens enjoy and should only be judged for to professional misconduct.

What's Your Point of View?

Question 2

Is it the nature of all governments to become corrupt?

Background

We have seen in modern history, instances where instruments of government were used to benefit a few at the expense of many. In some instances, government officials elected by popular support manifested this. Is this inevitable?

YES

Those that would say "yes," contend that power corrupts—and "absolute power corrupts absolutely" (Lord Acton).

NO

Those that would say "no" would argue that government is not intrinsically evil, but is an instrument that could be used for good depending on those who govern.

Now What's Your Point of View?

Question 3

Is a utopia a realistic endeavor?

Background

Utopia, the perfect society, where everything is equal and everyone gets along. Is this really possible?

Is it in human nature to be loving, kind, generous, and selfless? Is this something that can be maintained for decades or centuries? Will man suddenly become benevolent and less prone to greed, envy, or covetousness?

Should societies try to establish utopian societies in order to make the world a better place?

YES

Idealist may argue that it is a realistic endeavor, for societies to implement a utopian society. It would help men to learn how to share, look out for others, and it would eliminate the disparity of resources within social groups.

Furthermore, it would eliminate the conflict between religious factions for all religions would be abolished. The government would be responsible for everyone.

NO

Opponents of a utopian society argue that it is the nature of man to look out only or himself or herself. Therefore, it would be impossible to eliminate greed and selfishness from a utopian society. It is not a realistic endeavor to create such a society for it would be doomed to fail. The major flaw would be the nature of man, which would topple such a society.

Furthermore, they contend that the Garden of Eden was such a society and self-centeredness caused the society (made of two people) to fall.

Now What's Your Point of View?

Question 4

Is it cost efficient to create a welfare state?

Background

A welfare state is one in which a government ensures that all people are entitled to the basic services and resources regardless of their ability to provide it for themselves.

YES

Those that say "yes" would contend that people are more happy and healthy in a welfare state. Without it, people's circumstances are more stressful resulting in a greater emotional, mental, and financial cost.

NO

Those that say "no" would contend that a welfare state creates an unnatural dependency on the on the state and stifles the individual and new innovations.

Now What's Your Point of View?

Question 5

Should politicians stay in office for life?

Background

In many places around the world officials remain in office for lengthy periods, whether they are good officials or not. Should the United States adapt such a practice and allow all politicians to remain in office for life as they do Supreme Court Justices? Or is it important that new blood be infused into the political process to provide innovative insights and renewed energy?

YES

Politicians should remain in office for life because they have experience and maturity on their side. The more time they spend in the system the more they will be able to accomplish.

NO

Politicians should not remain in office for life. The more time they spend in office the lazier they become and the more they become part of the problem rather than the solution. More time in office, could increase the chances for them to become corrupt and fall prey to an incestuous system.

Now What's Your Point of View?

Question 6

Should a politician's family have a monopoly on political offices?

Background

In history power, status and position has been passed down from parent to child as evidenced in Egypt, Israel (King David to Solomon), and even in England today.

In the United States, the right to an office due to family linage and political influence is still at play although it may appear on the surface to be different. The Kennedy and the Bush families are prime examples of this tradition at work. Should political monopolies be allowed to exist while bank or corporate monopolies are publically, politically, and legally opposed?

YES

Advocates for this position argue that the people exercise their free will when they cast their ballots to elect a politician. Public servants are not forced upon citizens as in other places in the world. Therefore, by its very nature the process does not promote or foster political monopolies.

NO

Those against the position, argue that those who are well off, affluent, and who have strong political ties are the ones who can continually run for office, and sustain long term campaigning.

Therefore, they have name recognition, political influence, and have the wealth to advance their political aspirations, over a lesser-known individual.

Now What's Your Point of View?

*Politics is the art of looking for trouble, finding
it everywhere, diagnosing it incorrectly and
applying the wrong remedies.*

Groucho Marx

Idea Prompts

In this section (questions 7-10), you will be given a question for which **you are to gather the background information through research.** You are to identify the strongest arguments for each position and list it. Then you are to give your point of view.

Try to narrow down the **yes** and **no** position to one argument that reflects the general trend of each position—this will reduce confusion and the blurring of the issue.

In politics stupidity is not a handicap.

Napoleon Bonaparte

Politics have no relation to morals.

Niccolo Machiavelli

Question 7

Should individuals be required to have a political record of accomplishment before running for political office?

Background

YES

NO

Now What's Your Point of View?

Question 8
Should people make a career of holding political offices?

Background

YES

NO

Now What's Your Point of View?

Question 9

Should politicians attack the character of their opponents?

Background

YES

NO

Now What's Your Point of View?

Question 10
Can communism really work?

Background

YES

NO

Now What's Your Point of View?

CHAPTER 4

Topic

SELF-ASSESSMENT

*Suppose you like someone very much. Then, by a
familiar halo effect, you will also be prone to believe
many good things about that person - you will be biased
in their favor. Most of us like ourselves very much, and
that suffices to explain self-assessments that are biased
in a particular direction.*

Daniel Kahneman

● ● ●

Self-assessment is a critical part of debating. The ability to analyze your argument in light of new information honestly is key to expanding and sharpening your mind.

Self-assessment is used in many facets of life— like in public speaking or performing a job. The ability to self-assess can help you to make the best decisions for your life, school, family, and career. It is for this reason this chapter on self-assessment has been included in this book.

Do you know who you are? What you want to do? Do you like who you are? Are you persuaded to do things because others think it is best? Or are you in tune with your deep desires for your life? Do you make decisions because society says, "this is what you need to do?"

Self-assessment gives you freedom—to consider your feelings, thoughts, opinions or beliefs, to be yourself, and to explore your special interests, talents, dreams and desires. Self-assessment will help you to be courageous—for you are able to identify, confront, and devise a plan to overcome your fears and anxieties.

In essence, self-assessment helps you to unlock self-knowledge. And this will help you as you go through life whether it is preparing speeches, developing debate arguments or in making life decisions. At the root of it, is *you*—and *you* should be comfortable being *you*.

In this chapter, you will find several questions that you can tackle as a debate topic. Unlike in the previous chapters you will not be given background information on the issue.

Rather you will be given a positive side and a negative side to the question (prompts) that will help you start formulating your thoughts and opinion.

Our question list is not exhaustive; but it should give you a starting place for self-exploration. Remember you are free to be yourself—so be honest about how you feel or what you think about the issue.

If you are bound by societal beliefs, family expectations, or peer pressures allow yourself to shed them—this assessment is ***all about you***. (If you have questions that you would like to suggest please visit www.excusemeletmespeak.com and submit it through the contact center…just reference the book).

Question 1
Who am I?

I am...

I am not...

Question 2
What do I want to do with my life?

I want to...

I don't want to...

Question 3

What career is best for me? If you do not have a career, what do you want to do when you get older?

I want to do...

I don't want to do...

Question 4

When should I change careers? If you are not in a career now, think about what extracurricular activities are you interested in.

I like what I do...

I don't like what I do...

Debate Handbook

Question 5

What college do I want to go to?

I want to go to _____because...

I don't want to go to _____ because...

77

CHAPTER 5

Topic

CONCLUSION

Reasoning draws a conclusion, but does not make the conclusion certain, unless the mind discovers it by the path of experience.

Roger Bacon

My hope is that you continue to expand and sharpen your mind through debate. Find topics of discussion and gather information on both sides of the issue.

Then decide which position fits your point of view. Then engage people in a discussion and use those conversations as an opportunity to refine and strengthen your position—and to encourage others to expand their minds through debate.

Without activity, the mind is left dormant—because it is not being exercised. As with any muscle, your mind should be regularly exercised for it to grow in knowledge and be quick to analyze information.

As you go through life, take time to get to know yourself. Self-awareness is necessary if you want to truly be yourself. There are many who are followers or imitations of another person—they do things because others believe it is right. Living your life that way may seem easy and good but it is not free—it is giving someone else control to shape who you are.

You can agree with other people's assessment—but the decision to follow their suggestions or advice should be made because you see the benefit of following their counsel and not because you are pressured to do it. This will help you not to have regrets in life.

The exception being when it comes to following God, obeying your parents or those in authority over you.

Personal Story

When in high school my guidance counselor advised me to be a homemaker. He discouraged me from applying to colleges. He would not even give me the applications—because he did not believe I should apply. Why I do not know.

But I assessed my situation…I decided that I wanted to go to college because both my parents went to college and had gotten their Masters degrees, my friends were all applying to college, and I desired to do something great with my life.

I applied to several colleges without the help of my guidance counselor. I did get my BBA and my Masters. I am so thankful that I did not follow his advice because it was not right for me at that time. However, I did become a homemaker after I had achieved my college goals.

Some suggestions may be helpful but they are given in the wrong season of life.

My Hope for You

My earnest hope is that as you expand your mind in areas of debate that you will also do so in freedom—be yourself. Make decisions that are truly in line with your hearts desires... and your goals. If you are not sure what to do, then seek wise counsel—your parents, friends, a trusted advisor or God. There is benefit in a multitude of counselors for they will help you look at the issue from many angles and will help you to consider things that you did not previously consider.

If you would like to suggest debate topics, share your testimony, or offer feedback please go to www.excusemeletmespeak.com and submit your thoughts via our contact center (please place *Debate Handbook volume 1* in the subject line).

It's more fun to arrive a conclusion than to justify it.

Malcolm Forbes

www.ingramcontent.com/pod-product-compliance
Lightning Source LLC
Chambersburg PA
CBHW041104110426
42740CB00043B/148